T0196988

Falling Into Grace

S. M. STOLL

WESTBOW
PRESS®
A DIVISION OF THOMAS NELSON
& ZONDERVAN

This book is a work of non-fiction. Unless otherwise noted, the author and the publisher make no explicit guarantees as to the accuracy of the information contained in this book and in some cases, names of people and places have been altered to protect their privacy.

WestBow Press books may be ordered through booksellers or by contacting:

WestBow Press
A Division of Thomas Nelson & Zondervan
1663 Liberty Drive
Bloomington, IN 47403
www.westbowpress.com
844-714-3454

Because of the dynamic nature of the Internet, any web addresses or links contained in this book may have changed since publication and may no longer be valid. The views expressed in this work are solely those of the author and do not necessarily reflect the views of the publisher, and the publisher hereby disclaims any responsibility for them.

Any people depicted in stock imagery provided by Getty Images are models, and such images are being used for illustrative purposes only. Certain stock imagery © Getty Images.

Unless otherwise indicated, all Scripture taken from the King James Version of the Bible.

Scripture quotations marked (AMP) are taken from the Amplified Bible, Copyright © 1954, 1958, 1962, 1964, 1965, 1987 by The Lockman Foundation. Used by permission.

ISBN: 978-1-6642-8461-6 (sc)
ISBN: 978-1-6642-8463-0 (hc)
ISBN: 978-1-6642-8462-3 (e)

Library of Congress Control Number: 2022921614

Print information available on the last page.

WestBow Press rev. date: 02/01/2023

Dedication

These pages of testimony are dedicated to all-powerful, all-loving Almighty God in three persons. Each one is necessary to know as we move through life and as the world becomes a kaleidoscope of thoughts, images, actions, and reactions to the world around us and beyond our borders. He is ever teaching us His ways and revealing who He is and who we are that we might trust that He has a purpose for each person and each situation.

He can control and flow in every dimension of time and eternity. I thank Him that through the mystery of His plan and design, He is more than able to save us from our limitations of understanding his love through intervening for us in the threats and challenges of life in this dimension. He can reach through death to create new life through fear and doubt to create peace.

When we experience His interventions and find that he is faithful when we are yet unformed in our roles on this planet, we can push past our doubts about ourselves and His ultimate authority, to hope and believe that He is the Author and Finisher of our faith. As we are called to praying for His wisdom in the intervention of others, we must develop faith that as Ruler over all dimensions, He must do what His plan calls for for all creation—to cause rejoicing or to allow suffering—due to humankind's decisions, despite our objection and rebellion.

I have kept the angels busy trying to keep me from my carelessness and unwise decisions. I did not deserve to be saved, nor do we deserve His many miracles that we do not always credit to Him. Therefore I write in thankfulness for His love and mercy and give Him the glory. I thank Him for falling into grace.

I dedicate also to family He places in our lives, who love us, put up with us, and people who come into our lives as pieces of a puzzle that we may not recognize until the puzzle is complete.

Thank you, Terri, Annette, Justin, Jordan, Hayden, Elle, Silas, and Lux.

Preface

These pages have been recorded to bring remembrance for me, and for you, of what our Creator God does to bring us along a path and life course that will bring the miracle of Life to redeem us when we fall, physically or spiritually, and that will create trust for what eternity holds for us. I give them to His seekers as instructed by the One who created miracles all through my life and the One who creates them in you. Otherwise, I would hold them as treasures in my heart.

He is never finished perfecting and completing what He has ordained for us, whether we have attained heights of accomplishment in this dimension of time or hidden our talents under a bushel until it is lifted in faith in ourselves or crushed by the heel of our fears. The eternal surpasses time, and God let me experience crossing the limitations of time and space through a fall to my death and miracle healing, and visit to meet Jesus, to encourage you that God is real, heaven is real, and this dimension is where we prepare for life that is beyond imagination. However, the path to arriving is filled with temptations and trials of sickness and loss—walls too strong to climb over or break through on our own. We need to know if it is worth the struggle and is truly there.

Although my story is a portraiture from a fading era, and you may be looking for what holds the minds and interests of those investing in future developments in society and science for reality, I declare that love and truth and faith are reality, and are never outdated, and are critical elements for successful progress. Each generation receives challenges unique for each step upward. But if the steps are unstable, we lose the progress we hoped to gain. Our fall from the grace of God is difficult to overcome. Love never gives up helping us to overcome.

I submit this message to readers who are looking for true reality and hope.

Introduction

Time is a capsule that comes with our birth, to be taken each day with water to activate the life within us. Water comes from many sources and will influence what our lives will produce. It can bring health and blessing from the water of the Word of God, or it can bring sickness and loss of purpose by drinking contaminated water from deception and unhealthy desires that divert from our God-given goals and our destiny and indeed cause the abortion of who we were born to become.

God has placed his plan for us in that capsule, for it comes with directions on how we are to take it and use the power and promise within. It also comes with caution of misuse and the damage and death that can result. There are ingredients for energy, for health, and for wisdom to confront the challenges we will meet as we live and grow. We can have peace that the capsule was given in love, and we can trust the One who gave it. What cannot be trusted is receiving deception of its purpose on how to live in this measure of time. When we get confused about how and when to take the capsule, we need to make sure we read the label with the instructions once more.

> My frame was not hidden from You when I was made in secret, and skillfully wrought in the lowest parts of the earth. Your eyes saw my substance being yet unformed, and in your book they all were written, the days fashioned for me, when as yet there were none of them. (Psalm 139:15–16)

We are not an accident; we were put here deliberately, with time to grow into what was fashioned for us.

Even with instructions, we can want the power inside that capsule to be used for our own plans. We can use our will to decide our use of what is inside. God knows when we need to see into His kingdom to decide why time was created and to understand it.

The controversy that keeps pace with the ages concerns whether life is perishable or lives on. Acquiring and achieving forms of power, material treasures, fame, knowledge, and tastes of love available to us within time can persuade many of us that there are no greater treasures to be obtained and therefor only strive for them here. Or we can live without hope of arising from a meaningless and poverty-stricken existence unless we know beyond doubt that a higher dimension truly exists.

We can read and believe with faith that it exists, but hardship, pain, loss, and wars can dissolve faith and hope, and has potential to destroy society as we know it. When we know home is awaiting us in a dimension of completeness for us, then we can rejoice and face life as it comes to us. We can hold onto gods here for temporary satisfaction, but the God that we withhold ourselves from can make whole what is incomplete. But who is He?

Often, the God of Creation is to us a sculpted figure that comes from teachings or fears we have received throughout our lives. The sculpture must come alive. We may not have a clear vision of His character or the true atmosphere of where He lives in a kingdom beyond our grasp of reality. Sometimes, God makes a bridge across time to take us to where Truth lives. I crossed that bridge.

I write my witness to share with you the glory of Who I saw and the glory that heaven holds for us. I tasted the eternal dimension where love abides, where it is *home* to all who have crossed the barriers to find it is there waiting for us. However, there are requisites for going there and remaining there. The prophets record God's call to us to return, even when we have found Him and brought heaven down and have then strayed so far away that we lose the path that can lead us back to Him. He will create a path.

Falling into Grace

Have you ever, as a child, chased the sunshine to a cozy spot on the soft green grass and lay there stretched out—expectantly, patiently—sensing every vibration of the earth to feel it move in its orbit around the sun? Or have you, after a day of busy doings, waited for the sun to fade and darkness to descend with the promise of a star show as you gaze into a canopy of starry wonders? Did you project your soul and spirit in a path through them to explore the dimensions of the worlds beyond them? I have, and as someone who has been through near-death experience, NDE, I write to witness that it is real. Through the centuries, glimpses of the world beyond the stars have been seen. Yet those in the dimensions of this present world hold us prisoner for fear of getting lost in an illusion of people's accounts of these journeys. Discoveries that would deflect the tastes and smells of passions we desire to explore here on earth instead. When the accelerating scientific discoveries related to Earth are revealed, we hear and read of the excitement of plans on how to change the foundations of our world and cultures to suit our need for new forms of living.

God sends enlightenment to break through barriers to living a more abundant life, to be compatible with His will to transform our lives in a beneficial way. However, humankind can distort the purpose of these revelations. A light needs to be revealed on God's dimensions, which He longs for us to accept that we might discover a path so often disbelieved and rejected. If we throw away sublime treasure for the addicting flavors that are transitory, it will fade away. These are sandcastles that dissolve in the flooding tide of humanity. For that reason, I decided I would obey a command of long ago, when I arrived back from a journey that revealed to me the reality of the world beyond the starry sky that I so knew in my heart was true reality. I was told to give witness to what I had experienced so that humankind would come to believe that God is real and that heaven is real but that gravity to this world is real as well. Hate, anger, jealousy, and fear are real, clinging to this present darkness. A dark light sheds deceit.

The event I am to share is not unique; it comes from a shared experience of flesh and blood creations of God who, through the ages, were to be messengers of hope to a besieged humanity overcome with philosophies, ideologies, religions, and cultures containing both truth and deception. We are left to sort them out to find what is authentic. The truth is found in the light and love of a dimension to be found, unexpectedly, by most who are translated into it, sometimes by suffering and loss. There is the knowledge that it is there and is described in an ancient book of mystery and truth called the Holy Bible. It comes to those who experience it through the enigma of death, or entrance into it.

Some desire to be among the first to be on a spaceship journeying to the Moon or Mars. They do not fear leaving Mother Earth for an adventure to another realm. They are willing to pay large sums of money for the experience. Those who have a near-death experience pay with their lives, in one form or another, in exchange for a higher form of living—one that is clarified by being loved unconditionally and forgiven, and in turn forgiving others. They will use their faults and failures to forgive, returning with renewed purpose.

In 1980, my husband and I were preparing for a visit to my mother and brother in Sedona, Arizona, where they resided. We usually made the trip in alternate years. The location radiated with God's creative work in the sculptured formations in the Red Rocks. The spiritual atmosphere was only surpassed by family love: Mom with her delicious meals, Daddy with his dry humor and courage in battling cancer. My brother, Hal, and I spent hours discussing and debating until the morning hours. Friends Art, Fern, and Dave would come to play games around the dining room table, and Art entertained us with his poetry and humor. However, my special joy was to slip outside and take my Bible over the slope beyond the backyard fence.

Making my way past the juniper trees to a jutting

rock over the dry stream bed beneath, I would dangle my feet in the breathless joy of the special sense of God's presence and the view of the mountains on the way down the slope. Then, I would look down to see if I could spot the huge footprint of the local mountain lion that lived up the mountain on Chimney Rock. He came to check if there was a pool of water in the shallow basin. He was a laid-back fellow and came to visit the neighborhood from time to time.

Our neighbor Betty was hoisting the flag when she heard a stir over at the cactus a few yards away. There he lay as a spectator, and because she had no fear of God's creations besides that from wisdom, she looked at him, told him how beautiful he was, and continued her task. He got up and ambled away, having overseen his territory. Mom had mentioned earlier that she had seen a blond "kai-oh-tee" hanging around the back fence.

Daddy would not be with us this trip. Two years before was a time of loss and a time of gain for my father, who had received Christ Jesus as Lord and Savior of his life. He had experienced healing of tumors before his death, due to the Lord's mercy and grace, but he was tired from the long fight due to a heart worn out from chemotherapy. A few weeks later, he died quietly beside my mother, in his sleep, with a slight smile on his face. What he saw is only known to him. He had met the Lord, and it was the joy of his life to know His love and forgiveness.

He had a long, painful struggle in his life but developed overcoming determination. He had courage while overcoming being crippled at the age of sixteen. He and a friend had been playing near a railroad yard. They were crossing between the cars on the way home when the train began rolling forward and jolted my father off the tongue as it started up. His leg was severed, and the friend ran away to get help. Daddy dragged himself home. Dirt from the road impacted his severed leg and acted as a tourniquet.

Enduring the mocking of the schoolchildren, for there weren't any crippled children for them to relate to, and transitioning to different schools due to his father's career as a union carpenter, he left his school education to spend the rest of his life reading and learning. My mother was instrumental in building his confidence. He found his talents and enjoyed them. He played his fiddle and appeared on a local radio station. He loved to pan for gold in the waters of California and had a claim he worked for silver ore. His love for ghost towns and Spanish music, along with a passion for photography, caused him to fear dying. Cancer terrified him, as did leaving family, friends, and the adventure of living.

It took suffering, and finding new adventure in discovering Jesus, to cause him to long for the adventure beyond the sunny skies of his beloved West, for the starry heavens that beckoned him. He saw God's hand through miracles of healing but was impatient to put aside the loves of this life, along with his favorite truck, Sweet Pea.

The Holy Spirit had revealed to me that the trip we were to take would involve a life-changing event. I was tentatively curious as to what would have such an impact, but God had done so much in our lives two years before that there was an expectation of something special.

Before returning to my story, I realize I must record the rest of my father's story, which has greater miracles than my own, because of how long he battled for them, and for the forgiveness that brings about what God requires of us all but is not easily attained. There are those beloved souls of whom only God knows their true worth and perseverance to conquer life in their sphere of dwelling among private challenges.

Their trophies were not like those who had crossed the finish line ahead of them. Instead, they were held in the hand of God until crossing the finish line of this life, sometimes crawling in pain to cross the goal. He drank all God put into his cup, bitter or sweet. He loved people and animals—perhaps with a little more joy and devotion—and gave whatever it took to run life's race as a handicapped person whose riches were not in a bank. They were in family and adventuring in the mountains or the desert he loved, standing in admiration of a sunrise or sunset, laughing at the antics of the animals he watched with glee.

When my husband and I heard of Daddy's battle with cancer, we made a trip out to encourage and love him. He had not attended church, as he felt he wasn't worthy to attend, but there was a look in his eyes, and a gentleness, when he wasn't berating the unwise decisions of politicians and cruelties to people and animals, when you saw the seeking within. He wasn't afraid to be himself, or afraid of life, except for cancer. He knew his faults and debits, and I think he was concerned about crossing into unknown territory.

It was the era of the Charismatic visitation of the Holy Spirit and miracles. I felt born for it when standing in awe of what was witnessed and experienced.

My parents were surprised that their shy and timid daughter could be part of it. I was expecting God to grant them the joy of entering this new realm in this season and tasting the freedom that came from knowing Jesus and the Holy Spirit. Daddy needed the support of friends who would pray for him, visit him, help him, and believe for him. I found a Full Gospel meeting and finally convinced my parents to go.

They enjoyed the love and fellowship and were agreeable to attending church the next Sunday. Daddy was struggling within himself after the message, as an altar call was extended. It was a small group that evening of friendly, loving, and dedicated members. They were aware that Daddy needed Jesus, and he needed them. They waited compassionately while he agonized in battle. Standing next to him, I was feeling the battle and knew it would take strong prayer to break through his humility and defenses.

The atmosphere was alive with God's presence as the call was repeated four times in patient love. With an abrupt movement to step past me into the aisle, he stumbled forward, and heaven come down to meet him as he fell to his knees and was surrounded by caring members whose outpouring acceptance was life changing.

Later that week, while attending the church's

western fellowship, the Holy Spirit drew my attention to a lively personality enjoying those around him. He limped with a crippled leg. The Holy Spirit informed me that he was to be Daddy's friend to take him through the pain he suffered. I boldly came to him and told him what the Spirit had said. Being a visitor from Ohio, we had never met before. He looked amazed and was weighing this invitation to come meet my father. The next day, there was a knock on the door, and Art had accepted the invitation but was looking a little bewildered, which quickly left as he and my father bonded right away. His wife became my mother's best friend. Also, Art's friend came often to pray and become a loyal encourager.

One interesting request from the Holy Spirit was to go down to the creek after a pouring rain, for He had something we were to see. The family piled into the car and found a place to park under the trees while hearing the roar of the water. We walked over to the bank, observing the strange sight of the water being detained at the concrete walking bridge as water heaped high above the bridge. The bridge was almost dry, but water ran underneath. At the time, I did not link the significance to the path ahead for my father. God does things like that to remind us that Joshua and the Israelites crossed over on dry ground as the river was heaped above them. The flooded river couldn't sweep them away.

Another puzzle for my mother and I was walking into the sunroom where Father would gaze out the window across the little ravine to delight in the Red Rocks. We asked what he was watching so intently. He said, "the burning bush." We turned to look, and sure enough, a medium-size juniper was engulfed in a burning blaze yet remained the same. He said he had watched it for some time, but it never burned up, and there was a house across the road from it. Why was it not put out?

So we continued watching with him until we knew this was not normal. We decided to walk around the road to it. We were chatting and enjoying the walk until we reached the location. There was no burning bush or burned remains—only blackened berries from where a juniper should have been, but no ashes and no stump, only dry ground. We searched up down the road thinking we had missed the location, but nothing was found. A silence settled over us as we returned. We sensed a questionable deduction that Daddy was being "called."

Sometime later, I was praying on the floor of my living room, when the Holy Spirit said a strange word to me—"A volcano is rising in the west." I knew it was a message to be decoded, feeling it had to do with my father. Shortly after, there was a phone call from my mother that Daddy was suffering, with large tumors appearing over his body. He had given up on chemotherapy and its side effects and refused hospitalization.

She wanted me to come. There was a plea in her voice for "healing" prayer from me, and it shook me somewhat. It was a challenge to believe God would supernaturally heal my father when I, personally, was praying for him. The knowledge was there that healing was real, and I had witnessed it, but what would happen if I didn't believe enough, and he died. I could but trust that God was in control but was not sure about how the challenge would be met.

However, the Holy Spirit was ready for the challenge. He brought me to the Bible for training, for reading the healing scriptures and my faith in them. He would send me to one, and there would be a challenge from His firm command to believe what was written. He was not gentle with my hesitation of being challenged to step into those scriptures. He firmly asked, when reading the scripture, "*Do you believe that this is true?!"* Realizing this was serious faith, and I was being equipped for a mission, my response was positive. Another, and another, until we covered several. Finally feeling prepared, I still wondered if He would meet me there.

On the plane, I kept hearing in my heart, "This mountain will be removed, and cast into the sea." When the plane landed, the time had come to face what was ahead. My brother, Hal, came to pick me up, and as we entered the house, there was no surprise to find the "volcano" was real. It was a tumor perched upon his shoulder, lifting his shirt. It was shaped like a volcano. There were two large tumors likened to small fruit on his chest near his side. That evening, my mother was rubbing his back, and I was across the room by the bar in the kitchen, watching and chatting as she ministered to him. Mother needed a break and called me to take over. Walking over, my mind was repeating over and over, "This mountain will be removed and cast into the sea!"

While touching the tumor, my soul flinched when feeling the evil of cancer under my hands. It was alive and was devouring his flesh. But we cannot fear; it had been dealt with by Jesus on the cross. I ministered to him for a while and then returned to the kitchen to talk with them from there. In a brief time, Daddy called Mom back again for another turn. She went, touching his back, and an amazed look came upon her face. Her voice was a little shaky as she called quietly to me, "Shirley, will you come and rub his back?" The Holy Spirit was stirring within my heart, and there was the feeling that something was happening. When I sat down and touched his shoulder where the tumor perched, there was no volcano; it had disappeared.

We went to the chapel on the mountainside in Sedona, known for its fabulous view of the Red Rocks. We went to give thanks to God for His intervention. The Holy Spirit told me to walk up front to the extra-large Bible on the stand before the altar, and I was to read a scripture He had for us on that page. I found it right away.

> The Lord is my light, and my salvation; whom shall I fear? The Lord is the strength of my life; of whom shall I be afraid? When the wicked came against me to eat up my flesh, my enemies and foes, they stumbled and fell. (Psalm 27:1–3)

The next day, when walking into the kitchen with a clear view past the bar into the den, there was my father, standing by his chair, with the arm, with his left hand resting above his head, on the doorframe. There, to my shock and dismay, the tumor had reappeared, and Daddy must have felt it back. I fought my mind questioning how this could happen. God does not make mistakes. But doubt and fear can. So, while stretching my arm and hand toward the manifestation as an unreal image, his shirt dropped down, and no tumor remained. However, over the next few days, the same event occurred. Daddy never told me he knew the battle was being fought. But one day my mother walked up behind me, viewing the same phenomenon of the tumor reappearing. She gasped aloud, and Daddy turned dejectedly to say, "It's back, isn't it?!"

He had lost hope. I explained that he was not to accept it because it was an apparition of evil. I encouraged my mother that she had to confront it as I was to leave soon. So, Mother got brave and declared Jesus had healed him and paraded all evil spirits of disease and hatred before heaven as defeated. After that, they did not return.

There were other tumors to see go, sometimes the next day. There was one in his throat that he coughed up after prayer. The two larger ones on his chest, near his right side, were difficult to see leave.

However, he was not happy. There was fear that they would return and that prayer was not strong enough to overcome them. He had to sleep in his recliner as the two tumors on his chest hindered his resting in bed.

So, I challenged God's word on the scriptures on sleep. I remember getting on my knees on my bed and praying these scriptures. This continued for a few days until Mom called to me from the yard to come and look into the window on the front porch. There my father lay sleeping on the couch on his right side. It was the first time he slept off his recliner. The tumors were shrinking, but still he was not responsive to the healings.

I went to the Lord for answers why Daddy was not responding. The words "whipping boy!" were clearly spoken. So, calling the family to a conference, we sat on the floor around Daddy's chair. We were to recall, and admit, the wounds we had carried all our lives, and repent where needed, and let them go.

My father had suffered a lot, and he told how his parents would not stop for his dog when they were leaving in their truck to move to another town. He and his siblings sat in the back of the truck, crying and shouting for them to stop, and had to watch the dog running after the truck but could not catch up.

As Daddy worked on the farm and crawled up the rows gathering onions in the onion field, his dog would go ahead and search for snakes, as it was copperhead and rattlesnake country. He grieved for his pet and had many cruelties in life to forgive and forget. But he always was there for his parents, and everyone loved his mother and her winsome personality and grandpa's gentle nature.

My own forgiveness was required to forgive her. There was a blurred incident of a memory of her from my childhood while my mother was in the hospital. There was a judgmental attitude toward her.

Then revealing to my brother about resentment of his taking my babysitting money when taking care of four small, active children for over a year, every weekend, being only about eleven or twelve years old. He never had to repay me, but he was a wonderful brother, and I always loved him.

We released our hurts and ended up laughing at pranks that were perpetrated among us. I hate to think of all I have unintentionally wounded. We need the Lord's forgiveness. So Daddy was released and became relaxed and at peace, even with the pain.

Before going to my father when the tumors appeared, I had been praying at my home on my living room carpet for my father's healing. The Holy Spirit had said he would heal my father because of the prayers for healing, but if He were to take him afterward, would I still love Him? He said He would take him easy. I replied that yes, I would still love Him, and if God took him, and it was his time, there would be a praise funeral for all that God had done for him.

After returning home, about three or four weeks later, we got a call late in the night that my father had died in his sleep, next to her. His back was turned toward her, but when she looked over his shoulder, a faint smile was on his face. No cancer was detected, but his heart had just failed to beat. It had been damaged from chemotherapy. I had not thought to pray for his heart, but it was not needed. She said he had been so lonely for Jesus that he did not interact with her or my brother as much. He wanted to go home; he was tired from the lengthy battle. However, the battle brought Jesus into his life.

When we were planning to fly out, there was news from Mother that my father's brother, who was an atheist by choice, was coming to the funeral. He apparently had not been popular with a few of the family, as he had not visited the family more than a few times over the years and was on a different social level. He had not attended some other members' funerals, so why now? He respected and cared for my mother and father for how they handled their lives. Besides, he had been told of my father's battle with cancer and the miracles he had experienced. He wanted to know what that was all about.

He came and entered the house with his pipe in his hand. He had a remarkable resemblance to John Wayne. He was known as the John Wayne of the shipping lanes, as he was a sea captain for years, and his favorite place was the China Sea. He had the stature of John Wayne—he was tall, had a voice like his, and walked like him. I was not prepared for what the Holy Spirit did, as an anointing of God's love seemed to pour right into my head and heart from the Lord as he walked over to me. He was here for a reason. God planned it, and Daddy prayed for it.

We bonded immediately and tagged after one another his full time there. A hillside on Dry Creek had fabulous beauty, overlooking those famous Red

Rocks with white running through them. My brother knew the owner, and we had dug pine trees from there for the yard once. So, we discovered a large, circular, natural rock garden, hidden among the trees, and we fell in love with its uniqueness.

Uncle Hal was smitten with the location; the views were spectacular. We were daydreaming of living there. He had once lived in New York City and then on the seas of the world, which did not have these kinds of scenes, and we were enjoying adventuring. We fantasized of building our houses there and visiting one another. I was like a daughter to him, and he was my long-lost dear uncle, feeling like I had known him all my life. Daddy had asked God to bring his family to know Christ before he died. God was answering his prayer. However, it felt like a betrayal of my father for being so close to someone when a time of reverence was to be a gift for his memory. God knew love and family were needed for his brother's introduction to the love Jesus gives us, and Daddy's hope was for the brother he loved. He shared a family member Uncle Hal had not known and later a church family he had not known.

Praise funerals were a new concept to the church there, and when the church children heard about it, they wanted to come, and they got permission to get out of school to attend and be part of it.

The outdoor service was blessed with a gorgeous Sedona day. Afterward, we went inside the house to fellowship and sing as we sat around the room. Jackie, the pastor's wife, had brought her guitar to lead us in joyful celebration for a loved one's graduation, with honors for all he had overcome and cherished on this Earth. We were singing when the feeling came to sing Daddy's favorite song, and it was suggested. It was "Come and Go with Me to My Father's House." The way they did it there was to ask the person next to them if they would go with them to Father's house, until the circle had been completed.

When it got to Uncle Hal, he did not know what to say. He was taking everything in with wonder as in a foreign land. My friend was sitting on the floor by him, patting his hand, and the children loved this visit from "John Wayne." There was so much love, and the presence of the Lord, that he was feeling it. When he hesitated, the children began to cheer him on, begging him to go with them. A tear began to roll down his cheek, and he said he guessed he would go with them.

He got up and walked into the dining room behind us. Mom followed, as she was like a quiet stream of comfort for each of them. Before he left the next day, he wanted to know more about the Christian life and took a book of testimony with him. When I returned to Ohio, I received a short call from him. All he said was, "Kid, I'm going to be with you on the other side!" God plans all things and brings good from all things.

John 10:25b "The very works that I do by the power of My Father and in My Father's name bear witness concerning Me (they are my credentials and evidence in support of Me.) The Amplified Bible

We had a wonderful fellowship on the trip two years later with family and friends. Time was getting close to taking our flight home, and I was wondering about the event the Holy Spirit had mentioned. So, taking my Bible to meditate and evaluate the purpose

God had for us in making this journey across the map to Arizona, I was praying as usual in my favorite place when I was suddenly blindsided and surprised by an onslaught of fear. There was an aggressive attack from a spirit of evil and premonition of falling into the black darkness of the grave. The very real threat was being dropped like a blanket over my whole being. It was menacing and gripping me as firmly as a physical force. Its name was unmistakable—death. There was no question of whom it was intended—*me*. I struggled spiritually with it, but it clung and would not let go, and there was no breaking its hold. My neighbor, who had been in Vietnam, once told of his feeling when entering battle—that you realize someone wants to kill you—and that feeling was real at that moment.

I was desperately pleading into the azure blue sky for my Lord to send help when a misty vision of a man's face that I did not recognize appeared, and his name came with it. Never having met the man but having heard of him when my daughter, a few years earlier, had visited his ministry in Yuma to determine if God wanted her there, it was a shock to have seen this unfamiliar face in the sky. Since hearing he was a strong man of God, I prayed for God to send him to pray for me.

While still amid my struggle, my mother's head popped over the hill. She said the man in the vision had called our evangelist friend to inquire if something was wrong in our family. Becoming stunned by the quick answer to prayer, however, I called out to her to say, "Yes, for it is a matter of life and death!" Moments later, faith appeared, and the presence of death disappeared. My mother inquired what it was all about, but there was a restraint from telling her as there was no reason to frighten her. What was important was the freedom from fear as someone would be praying against death.

The next day, we were to climax our trip with a picnic and hike up the canyon to West Fork. Beginning the hike, we came to the abutment of the burned down swinging bridge that had led to the lodge where Zane Grey had written *The Call of The Canyon*. We made our way down the slope to Oak Creek, which was dry in that section, but we found a deep pool farther down the creek. I rolled up my slacks to wade. As we ended our time there, the family wandered around in the area where there was an old orchard and the remains of the fireplace.

As quickly as the spirit of death had come upon me, the spirit of overwhelming joy and expectation enveloped me, so there was an overpowering urge to run ahead, up the slope to the swinging bridge abutment. The road to the car was a short distance up the steps from there. Not knowing why there was a rush to go ahead, it was as though there was an urge to climb the mountain slope.

When reaching the small abutment, about ten feet or more above the creek bed, and while stepping onto the platform, out from under the rock step, a coral-colored snake came slithering toward me. When stamping my foot, it ran back under the rock. It looked poisonous, but later I heard it was a mountain snake and was not harmful. While victoriously and loudly proclaiming that death had missed his chance, a wind began to stir up, and losing my balance, I fell back, and while getting to my feet, was beginning to lose balance once more. Backing up from the snake had brought me to the edge of the abutment. Incredibly, while knowing that when standing up in that strong breeze, I would go over, there was no fear. The intercession for me was working. He was praying. Then pivoting around to see my family below before going over, the scene was as one of horror, for they were riveted, looking up, like speechless stone statues.

Knowing the chances of being killed or injured badly on those boulders and rocks, but for God's deliverance, there was remembrance of God's Word that promised that His everlasting arms were under us. So, when beginning to fall, that promise was trusted. While stretching my arms out, repeating the scripture, believing that truly His everlasting arms were there, my feet began to leave the abutment.

While looking down at the rock-strewn creek bed, there was incredible realization of a thin silver tunnel of light beginning to wind its way upward toward me as if in an amazing script. It gently wrapped itself under my outstretched left arm, around, and under my back. I was instantly translated out of the present dimension into a heavenly dimension. When experiencing the current Charismatic revival at the time in 1980, it was not unusual for the supernatural to become a familiar realm when one had received the Holy Spirit and was introduced into the atmosphere of the eternal. Healings seemed a natural occurrence from a God who created all creation. However, God is much more than a healer; He has many names and governs all things, and I was to recognize that.

The reality of that dimension was far beyond the gifts of the Spirit and was a time of awe to realize

I had crossed the limitations of time and space, experiencing both being without a physical body but being within my spirit body and delighting to behold the glory of that realm. Belief prepares us for the incredible and secures us in the awesome glory of an Almighty Power, in whom we have learned to trust. However, this was almost like visiting, and being enveloped into a scene from Narnia where the impossible and anything supernatural can happen.

The magnitude of the supernatural peace, the triumphant joy, and the love that saturates and engulfs your whole being cannot be described. It is intimate to a degree that possesses your heart in a love so intense that it transforms your spirit, and you become one with it. The magnificent, beautiful light of living love, peace, and joy that engulfed me while seemingly making me part of that dimension was a misty, softly swirling cloud of inconceivable brilliance, softened and intermingled with an activated pink, living swirl within that seemed to have a personality. It emanated love. There was awareness that it was alive and was softly whispering a warm welcome.

I also became aware that a figure was emanating from these clouds of glory. There was the incredible realization that the figure was Jesus manifesting before my eyes. He appeared as the Jesus I knew before time, and as in pictures of his life here on earth. Also, He appeared as my Savior, smiling in welcome, familiar in personality as Son of Man, however, bearing the majesty of the Son of God. Yet I saw Him almost like the Jesus who walked the earth with His disciples, fellowshipping with them, and wearing a robe identifiable to the pictures I was familiar with. However, there was the undeniable governing power and victorious confidence that made me, at that moment, in that dimension, understand that Satan and evil were no match for Him. I felt Him exercise an undefeatable power for me, that I might understand there was no reason to fear the future. He has no competition, even if we question why Satan's evil seems overpowering.

Now, as I write this, I realize it was part of why I was taken there—to overcome my fear and anger of evil, as in this time frame the ungodliness, greed, and struggle for power seems to be winning so many battles as we learn of the persecution, the brutality, the lies, and the deception, even within the church itself. We can let the world fade our remembrance of His supremacy, and that was one reason I had to write my testimony, not just for you, but for me to crystalize that He has no equal, no challenge too great. When I remember, I seem to be back there once again. He was so *real* and is so *real*.

A friend gave me a picture that had been painted by someone who had seen Him as I did. Others who encountered NDE have seen Him differently, or as a blinding light of love and power. I believe he appears in whatever form that will verify that He exists and is how He needs to reveal Himself to you. Some want to know from NDE people, what color are His eyes? I did not look into His eyes for being overcome with both the familiarity and majesty He exuded. It would not matter to me. He was there in my childhood and always there in times of joy, in times of trouble, when fear was prevailing, and I called for Him to save me. Especially when I felt invisible to the world of expectation and did not measure up. His love was also discipline to keep us safe, and I knew Him for that as it saved my life many times.

Not only our vision of Him, but our relationship to Him, or lack of it, is individual and special to each of us. He wants us to know Him as He relates to our place in time and our purpose on earth. We need to grasp the importance to our unity with this earthly existence and to the eternal of which we aren't always aware. We learn here, we decide here, we build a bridge here in our lives to God and to one another if we accept that blueprint for our lives, using building blocks of an eternal kingdom. We must become aware that self desires to build a bridge to this world of building blocks that are insecure and will lead to the collapse of what we desire to construct. The blueprint must be followed by its heavenly design and help us to reconstruct our lives when we fail and when we rise and believe in the architect. A child reassembles his Legos when what he builds needs reconstruction, so we must often go through some reconstruction throughout our lives. The architect understands and put clauses in the blueprint for that purpose when we call upon Him.

Most who experience this dimension know it is home and is where they belong, and know he is there, waiting for us. His smile holds heaven and is embedded in remembrance as it held me in a loving embrace and an almost teasing invitation and a question left to ponder, as He knew I was to return soon. "If you return to me, You can know whatever you want to know." When he offered that information, there appeared a misty form behind His left shoulder. It was a building and imposed upon my mind that it was a library. Others have seen the library, although there must be many there.

I didn't see angels, or venture into the unspeakable grandeur of heaven with celestial guides. It was not yet my time to enter the gates of heaven. The Holy Spirit had informed me that something would change my life, but there would be a return. The need was to see Jesus, who was personal, and to see Him for the purpose and message, later learning why the question and the caution. There needed to be a visual of why the importance of the covenant is to be kept within our hearts to obey what it asks of us. It was to be related as well as remembered.

I was not there long because of prayer, and because that was in His prepared plan. Then there was the strange experience of being inserted back into a body that had had no pulse, like a video of the visit to become stored in my mind and become part of me. Audio had been turned off to this world's sounds until hearing the anguish of my mother's weeping, and my husband's groans of disbelieving agony was like static in the vibrations of the glory of what I had witnessed. Then everything became clear, and I was returned to earth.

I was propped up against my brother's chest, hearing his quietly pleading prayer in a shaky but trusting voice, "God, please give my sister back." I was not on this dimension's wavelength, but still on heaven's, and there was no response to their shock of pain and loss because of the joy of seeing and being in the supernatural realm with Jesus.

My eyes opened to witness my propped up legs bearing a vertical wound from knee to ankle, with a spot of white bone near the ankle. There was no pain, only overwhelming joy. Then came the clear, commanding words from Jesus, spoken as a message to my heart, to be added and lived, from the never to be forgotten visit: "I have healed you, that you might climb this mountain to be a witness for me."

Since being told to climb the mountain to be a witness and feeling this was the time to obey and start, I got up on my feet and started a "running climb" up the mountain without alerting the family. They were too stunned to follow me while unable to absorb what they were witnessing. They were terrified to see me "foolishly" exercising my body after my fall and experiencing what they had observed was death. They had no inkling of the power of restoration received and the joy of being with Jesus while my body lay bleeding and lifeless on the rock-strewn creek bed. Nor did they comprehend the miracle was for their faith and for others who would hear. I continued climbing, while dimly hearing their shocked voices shouting for me to stop, as they determined that I had to be taken to a hospital. Not emotionally back in this dimension, compassion was absent to comfort them in the trauma of what they had experienced. My mind and my heart were still in the heavenly kingdom, still with Jesus.

I kept climbing on supernatural energy until the road where the car was parked was reached. When they caught up, they found me standing by the back door of Mom's new little Thunderbird that she was so proud of and for which she had saved for so many years. There was the instinct to wait, as my clothes had blood on them, and not wanting to ruin her new seats. Mom told me the rocks had blood also. At last I was becoming aware of this everyday reality that we deal with here on earth—to consider others.

The car seats did not matter to my mother; she wanted to get me to a hospital. I declined and resisted going against the miracle of being saved from injury and death, knowing Jesus had a purpose, unknown to me, for my healing, and there was a desire for it to be fulfilled. There was no need to be concerned about the blood continuing to flow. My gentle but "strong in faith" brother had prayed for it to stop while lying against his chest, and it stopped. He had a healing gift he used frequently at a healing ministry. You must remember that these were the days of God's visitations during the Charismatic revival. They are coming again, and we are to look for them and believe for them.

They could not understand the lack of pain or the miracle they had witnessed. That did not prevent my chattering away about meeting Jesus as we maneuvered down the winding road through Oak Creek Canyon, to find a little clinic along the way tucked away outside of Sedona. My husband and brother left the car with Mom and me remaining inside while they walked numbly across the dusty lawn to get someone to bring me inside. They soon came out after finding that the doctor had left for the day. Of course, God had provided for that, as a long brown and tan station wagon hurriedly arrived, driving up to the building, kicking up the dust. The doctor got out to speak with my husband and brother, then ran inside to reappear momentarily with a large wet bath towel. While walking toward the office with Mom clinging to my arm as though I might drop over, he hurried over to put the towel around my leg to wipe off the blood and see the injury. When he removed the towel, he was shocked to see there was no wound. He was very startled but led me into the office.

During the examination and probing to see if the skull had been penetrated after falling ten or more feet, while suturing the wound, it was repeated over and over that Jesus had saved me. There was no urge to tell him what had happened in the short while there in another realm, and being told there had been no pulse, for my husband had not admitted to him there was no pulse, and the doctor presumed there was unconsciousness for a few minutes yet was amazed I showed no signs of trauma. Knowing that if the doctor was told the truth, most doctors did not react to these kinds of NDE incidents with belief because of witnessing so many patients dying with horrific pain and terminal diseases. Why should God's hand redeem these people to receive special treatment? That is an answer only God knows. Maybe because it will turn our lives, and others, around to show us His desire for how we should live when we forget to return, when we have forgotten what we owe to others to tell of His almighty love and power, and not to give up believing in the wonder of miracles, for we are to pray for them.

He treated me with gentleness and kindness, and there was realization he had been chosen for this day in my life. The doctor examined my cognizance and reported my knowledge of being aware of the day and time. He proceeded to take an instrument to look into my eyes for damage from the fall, and there will always be the recollection of his reaction, and mine, because of what he observed. Wondering how the miracle would be believed, there needed to be confirmation, and for Jesus to impress this little insignificant being that He could choose anyone for His works and wonders.

This tall and lanky doctor, clad in blue jeans, had brought the little stool on which he was sitting, close to the cot where I had begun to sit up. Placing the instrument close to his eyes, suddenly he pushed back hard, on long lean legs, exclaiming, "This is amazing! This is amazing!" There was the stirring in victory exalting within me, and a smile of knowing softly touched my lips, when asking what he had detected. "There is light in your eyes!" he exclaimed. With that, a leap of joy was felt down in my belly, as if a living spirit lived in me. Then a peace began to settle over me. Jesus had authorized this work of glory for those who would hear, and to eliminate my doubt that this could have happened to someone so inconsequential, and who could have doubted had there not been this confirmation of what was both heard and felt. My witness of having been on the threshold of heaven was being confirmed by having brought back a little of the glory within my eyes. It was a gift from Jesus to call me back to Himself.

The doctor was still shaken when I mentioned my elbow had started throbbing and probably needed attention. He just shook his head as if not understanding what he had just experienced. He was exhausted from a long day and the surprises. He just said, "Come back in the morning."

We left for home, but the visit to the clinic was not acceptable to my family. What if the examination had fallen short of detecting unknown injuries? They thought more examination was needed to check for damage to internal organs. There was no understanding of why he had not called an ambulance and had further testing. Knowing the persistence of the medical profession to be sure of the patient's condition, I knew God had sent me to a place where my birthing stages of witnessing would not be lost. Instead, it was verified. My mother came to believe and rejoice in Jesus healing the injuries except for my complaining elbow, which the Lord had purpose to give caution for future testing. My mother took on her motherly duties when we arrived home, and she put me to bed. There, doubt of my worth to experience such a supernatural glimpse of the eternal was like fighting doubt, as I had fought with the spirit of death.

Heat enveloped me as I fought to hold onto Jesus and the dimension I hoped to return to. The profound love, peace, and joy, could not be denied. The reality of that dimension and of meeting Jesus face-to-face was undeniable, so victory was established once more. But doubt never gives up accusing us of our weakness and worthlessness. He knows every slip of the tongue, every person or deed we judged ourselves to be above committing the same misdeeds. That draws us away from God, fearing His disapproval or punishment.

My handsome brother came in to pray with me, and the pain left my elbow. But the complaining elbow was needed for this moment of prayer to become a moment of warning not easily forgotten. My brother Hal gave me a Word from the Lord that although overcoming this fall, there could be one that would be hard to climb up from.

Art, a dear elderly friend of the family, limped in to see and pray for the miracle child, as he referred to me. He was a combination of homegrown poetry and a love for the classics that he recited as often as the chance came up. I loved to hear him reminisce of western dramas until one could almost relive the history of the Old West as we sat in the shade of the mulberry tree, and the breeze seemed to resonate with the ghosts of the distant clash of battles, the victories, the losses, and the mourning of whispering voices whose broken hearts would haunt the desert lands and rocky mountains as long as time remained. He recalled bringing herds of cattle down from Flagstaff through the barren valley of Sedona of long ago. He had been an extra cowboy in a Wallace Berry movie and told of all the movies made in the area and of seeing John Wayne riding through the land before the real estate developers moved in.

He had a heart of love for everyone except for a mine boss when he worked in the mines in his younger days. The mine boss apparently was a detestable man who had injured in some way, or killed, Art's Indian friend "Little Joe." Art wrestled with his conscience and finally decided to kill the boss in revenge for all the harm and pain he had brought about in the mines. The Lord knew his heart and sent a vision right before his eyes. It was so real he could have touched what was there before him. He cried when he humbly related it. He saw an altar covered with a crimson robe, with an open Bible on it. A scripture that was alive, and revealing his own sin, was there for him to read, and it penetrated his heart.

After repenting and forgiving, peace descended, and the hate was gone.

When humbly receiving faith in my translation to a supernatural dimension, and was mine to keep forever, there was excitement to return home and begin to witness as Jesus had instructed. But first was another appointment with the doctor. When entering his office swinging a healthy elbow, I was met with a radiant smile. He gratefully explained that had I not walked in without injury, he could have lost his license for not sending for an ambulance to take me to the hospital for more evaluation. He was relieved, and not surprised, to see a full recovery, and he seemingly knew that what he had seen was a miracle. When we were leaving, his nurse asked if I had fallen from the abutment at West Fork, and with widening eyes, she stated that it had been a miracle. He handed me a report that verified the fall and that stated, "well enough to fly home the following day." My primary physician was to follow up when arriving home. On the report, something was revealed that had not greatly been a concern before. Something that would sometime later give God continued glory.

There was a significant thyroid nodule, which would be another miracle after being diagnosed later, three times, that it was cancer.

One night, I was standing in the bathroom looking into the mirror in a mood of relinquishment after determining there had been a maximum of healings and blessings for one person. The Holy Spirit asked if I was accepting it. Considering that question for a moment, there was a puzzled reaction. Had I not experienced my quota of miracles? If He was seriously expecting agreement, and that if this was God's will that it was to be rejected, then there was a family and people yet to love and pray for. The answer was no, I would not, for that seemed to be what He wanted to hear. The nodule had been extremely hard, and that convinced the medical profession it was cancer; also, there was the clicking of an instrument on my throat, and the physician tensed up, quietly evaluating that it was cancer. I got up in the night after my encounter with the Lord and was extremely sick and dizzy. When waking the next morning and touching my throat, I found that the nodule was very soft. It was obvious that the chemistry had been changed, and the nodule was no longer cancerous. The Lord informed me that there was still to be surgery, which didn't seem to make sense. He could have removed it unless there was another reason for the surgery; however, it was changed to benign. I was shown a vision of the surgeon who was to perform the surgery. He was fairly tall with dark hair and was wearing a long white surgical gown that stood out as if starched heavily. That gown puzzled me; I had never seen a surgical gown starched to that degree, but I realized later that it was for positive identification.

The confidence remained, even when taking the preparation for the surgery, becoming relaxed and sure when predicting to the disbelieving medical staff that there would be no cancer. They seemed to feel that this patient was unable to face the reality and smiled when trying to help me accept the diagnosis. My husband could not believe my vision of the doctor, and when walking up the sidewalk into the doctor's office for the first time after being chosen by my primary doctor, he kidded about the impossible knowledge of the doctor's profile. That was a lot of spiritual mystery for him to receive at the prospect of seeing that same profile. We were sitting on a couch where he could see into the receptionist window; however, it was blocked from me. After hearing the doctor's voice at the window, then came my husband's surprised admission, "Well, there's your doctor." He saw the proof of the vision. The doctor did not react in disbelief when told that I had been shown a vision of seeing his starched gown, and he laughed. It was probably a concession to comfort me, as cancer isn't easily accepted.

Before surgery, I was still proclaiming a benign tumor, but they were not accepting it. The anesthesiologist was very interested in my persuasion and listened in anticipation to see the results of the surgery. After waking from surgery and opening my eyes, he was smiling from across the room, sending a thumbs-up. When he came to the hospital room, he wanted to hear about what God had done. God apparently wanted him to believe in Him and in miracles. Another reason for the surgery was when my Christian doctor came in praising God, for she had been certain it was cancer. We were rejoicing in what God can do, and a very disagreeable woman sharing the hospital room heard the discussion. When speaking to her upon arrival into the room, I had inquired if she would like prayer. However, she got angry and rejected it with a curse. When my doctor left, a quiet and meek voice dared to ask if I would please pray for her. She then wanted to hear about God's love, when we don't understand Him or our lives. God must have wanted her to receive prayer very much for me to have a surgery that need not have happened. It must have been critical to her soul's survival. Someone had to stand in the gap.

The other reason was for the surgeon. The Holy Spirit informed me that the doctor would be delayed in coming to the office for his appointments after surgery, and there was the assignment to speak to a patient who would be waiting for her appointment. The surgeon had truly been delayed. A woman was anxiously pacing the porch where we had gone outside waiting to be called. She was trying to avoid people. I managed to stand beside her and start a conversation. She finally admitted to having had a life-after-death experience, and she had been a church person, and now she didn't feel the same about church as before. It was a confirmation as to my own question of why something had changed. My faith was deeper, and the Bible verified, but seeing a love beyond anything we have ever experienced concerning loving one another in the world or even in church makes one realize that it takes the Holy Spirit living within us to change our love to agape love. Love must live with Truth, and we wrestle with living with Truth and love, for we are not always sure that God loves us or that we deserve His love. Human love can be misguided and is but a shadow of God's love. Self wants to decide who to love and how to love, and the written Word must become a living Word, and it comes by seeing Jesus in our heart, who *is* the Word and Truth, letting Him love through us. The church is being shaped by God's hand, and we must let Him mold us while we struggle to return and "know everything we want to know."

I was the last to see the surgeon, and he was exhausted, pale, and shaky. I inquired as to what had happened. He sighed and looked down as he told of the previous surgery. She was a mother of several children. He inserted the scalpel, and her cancerous deterioration was overwhelming to the point that he had to just sew her up. There was nothing they could do. Here I sat before him, having survived the threat of cancer through God's hand, and I felt he was a little angry with God, and with me, for being redeemed when others did not have the same outcome.

The Holy Spirit revealed that it was necessary to intercede for this doctor and other physicians, as they saw so much heartache and bore responsibility to save lives, which they could not always do. We think of them as successful and admired, but they pay a high price for their gifts and years of education and skill to perfect them.

Hugs and goodbyes, and now with a believing and enthusiastic husband, we took a flight back home. He was willing to excitedly share the miracle with passengers sitting near us. Strangers were receiving because of his excitement and my sitting there with a bandage on my head. However, the world does not always receive our testimonies, especially to the auto workers he was so excited to tell that heaven is real. They had never known him to speak of spiritual things when baseball, basketball, and football were his usual topics. They did not recognize this exposition, and they wounded him with criticism and unbelief. But God had done a deep work in him inwardly, as he was a witness of steadfast devotion to his family, and he liked talking to strangers more than before. I realize that while my head was still in a realm where the eternal was so real, my big, handsome, and protective husband brought his thankfulness to live in a deeper understanding of the planet we live on and the lives of people and their decisions. My friends wanted to come to him about their problems for his insight and wisdom of human nature. I'm glad he chose to serve God with integrity and love of life here. Now he resides in the reality of eternal love and peace, as he has crossed over. He now shares my witness of heaven being real.

Returning home has somewhat faded in my memory. We didn't know how family and friends were going to relate to such a challenge to their commonsense minds and the stretch in our daily lives and simplicity in living. As I recall, our lovely daughters were shocked and surprised at the event. They believe it happened, but I'm sure they wondered how this *Star Trek* event could have occurred to our family. This was material for a sci-fi movie, and their mom wasn't a fan of them. For them, life was the reality of what their future roles were here on earth. They were going through their teen-aged growing pains and transition to "life beyond" on this planet. However, they always supported me and were believers. I remember their delight in telling their friends, and our youngest parading them in to see the bandage on my head, which proved I had fallen and lived to tell it.

There was some perception to feel a strange difference about church, which had been greatly loved and a rock in my life. Not what I believed or read in the Bible, or the fellowship, but as knowing there were developing degrees of understanding, truth, and love that revealed a grace we had yet to experience. We were to seek them as promised in God's Word. However, it was beyond the precious gifts and fruits of the Spirit that are blessing and filling, yet beckoning seekers to climb upward on Jacob's ladder into the knowing of His name, and the changing of our own.

While we grow, we feel the sculpting within our souls as the Spirit of God cuts away moldings of influences that create self-image, along with the desire to follow a path we carve out in the dusty ground before us. Our planned path can be lost from being realized as we become distracted by responsibilities that we allow to grow out of proportion.

My spontaneous reaction to the discovery that I

had seen the reality of my faith, and it was so real, so true, was probably, to those who would listen, like being drenched with a rushing stream of zeal. God used it and probably was a little amused by it.

When told that I would experience an event that would change my life, there was the assurance of returning to earth. That had been confided to our dedicated and vivacious choir director before leaving. Tilly could scarcely contain her excitement when I walked in with a bandage on my head and a mystery to be learned and shared that the event had happened. The pastor was not there the evening I returned, so Tilly spoke to someone in charge and asked if the witness might be given. Had the pastor been there, he probably would have held off until he heard it first to decide if it should be given. That would have been the wise decision; however, God does not always go by our decisions when He knows what will bring the best results—like my not being sent to a hospital when I could have believed man rather than God and wasted a miracle experience that was part of my purpose. Jesus knew it was to be given while my confidence was at its peak. He knew the reluctance to face crowds could have persuaded me to fear giving it when the anointing had faded.

God's wisdom is above, and greater, than man's wisdom.

It was time for the inserted record of the event to be replayed. There was an awed response. One visitor asked that I might relate the testimony to all six women's circles at her church. There were invitations from a couple of churches and two speaking invitations from women's fellowships.

The first was met with an anointing and the strong presence of the Holy Spirit. The prayer line was long, and Jesus was there to dispense mercy and grace. The next invitation was extended due to the first meeting and hopes for a repeat of the miracle message. However, it was not in God's plan; He knew what was needed. The message the Holy Spirit gave me was on the "Living Cross," which I'm sure did not sound uplifting to the board, and it was obvious that it did not meet with their approval, as sensed upon my arrival.

It was an illustration of how our human crosses work to conform us to the image of Christ and how they are preparing us to accept and fulfill our purpose in this dimension to translate us to an eternal home in God's dimension. The vertical beam represents our faith in God and His Word that points upward to the kingdom of God. The cross beam represents our lives on this horizonal plane of both blessings and battles with sickness and sin. Self, with its doubts and rebellion, is crushed in the apex of those beams as Christ Jesus overcame the world and the grave. The message was an extension of the first, giving credit to the greatest of miracles.

Before the meeting began, the Holy Spirit had preordered an encouraging soul to give me confidence while speaking. He was a disgruntled young man who apparently was compelled by an older lady, whom he loved and respected, to come with her to hear my miracle experience. It seemed that was not what he hoped to hear, as he made his discomfort known by restlessness and a frown. He wasn't looking for entertainment. The Holy Spirit gave encouragement to approach him to ask for prayer as I gave my message. He accepted with almost an excitement as he immediately took his chair to the back of the room and turned it around to straddle it like a smiling liberator. He was exactly what I needed. He smiled and nodded in agreement all through the message.

I saw the disappointment on the faces of the staff but acceptance by the audience, and one man had an illuminated understanding and cried out in joy. A lady pastor invited me to speak at a six-week seminar at her church, and I debated a few days and declined. The undesirable reception of the leaders of the women's fellowship caused a spirit of fear to pervade to my stepping out into a spotlight. I closed the doors the Holy Spirit had opened I felt it might cause problems in my home life by dividing my time with the needs of my family. Not realizing it at the time, I had also closed the door on publishing a manuscript of importance, which I spent three years writing as directed by the Holy Spirit. I had no credentials or resume of public speaking to give credit as an unknown author. I write this as a sad witness to the fact we are not to be irresponsible to value and use the gifts God gives us. Witnessing publicly would have overcome my fear, and God would have worked things out with my family. I was meant to be a bridge between heaven and earth.

There were years of intermittent witnessing as the Holy Spirit directed but knowing not to deliberately impose my testimony without His nudge. There was a visitation to a church and a Bible class of a few women, when a question came up that I had to truthfully answer by giving witness. Since I was a stranger, there was discomfort in obeying the strong urging of the Holy Spirit to speak out, but obedience is of God. There was a shocked quiet after I gave my witness, which caused me to question if this stranger might have offended them. I called the pastor the next day to explain not continuing to attend the class, as I was sent there for that witness, and it was for God and not myself. He understood and said my disclosing it had a strong impact on the women, so I knew it was meant for someone.

The nudge often came on airplanes, to those seated next to me. It was as though they knew there was a reason for my being seated by them and there was something they needed to hear. There was the man who came to work on the dryer, discussion and witness with an insurance man while making a routine call, and a woman on a plane who seemed excited to hear something especially important for her to learn, even as she sat down beside me. I especially remember one man who came stumbling down the aisle of a sparsely seated airliner. The attendant suggested we could sit wherever we liked and did not have to sit in our assigned seats. I was reading and hoped he would take any other seat except the one next to me. However, he sat down, as it was his assigned seat, and then began, in frustration, to confide he was going to retrieve his teenaged daughter, who had been put into jail for shoplifting. She had run away from home, and he knew she would resist returning with him. He didn't know what to do, and he was angry and overwhelmed. He was spilling out desperate emotions because he thought I was a minister because of the Bible in my lap. We talked, and he calmed down to accept prayer for the situation and for his daughter to be willing to return home with him. My witness and fellowship led him to accepting the life of a believer in Jesus, procuring the saving grace he needed to know how to pray and deal with his fractured relationship with his daughter and perhaps others in his family. He related, in some awe, that he had booked with another airline, but at the last minute he called American, and he knew not why. His eyes grew wide with wonder of how God had planned to have his life changed and retrieve his daughter without anger and unforgiveness.

Love was the answer and is so often why the lack of it causes so much anguish. It has many forms and works with other needed elements according to the situations. God works in the name of "I Am," and we cannot put Him in a box on how He deals with our problems. How precious to watch the restoring power of His wisdom and grace in dealing with His creation. Witnessing to that power of love and protection from evil is so amazing that people often doubt that it is real. Coincidence is their justification for disbelieving.

We don't realize how much He wants to be a part of our lives and see us blessed and flourishing. However, humankind too often chooses to temporarily flourish under a deceptive force.

I became concerned that repeating my story of the miracles in my life over and over, was creating pride and challenge from those who had not had a visit to see Jesus. I began retiring little by little and enjoying home, family, and my husband's retirement. After my husband died of a heart attack, I was unprepared because he handled all our affairs. Being given responsibilities, there was a need to accept and handle the challenges myself. What was not realized was that pride wanted control. The Holy Spirit wanted to guide me; however, I decided not to dodge what others were going through on their own. Avoiding witnessing to escape pride brought me to combat a greater pride. There was the trap of thinking our business affairs are solely our responsibility and the lure of being successful on our own in our endeavors. When we give our life to God, we cannot become double-minded and must let Him lead us into unfamiliar territory.

There were still daily devotions and a time of reading the Bible and sermons, but my mind was cluttered with family and responsibilities. It was allowing myself to divert from the path laid out for me. When we lose trusting His intervention in our affairs, we are open to the forces of evil. I lost my confidence and became fearful. Fear separates us from the presence of the Lord.

I had stepped over a cliff and was falling as my brother's word from the Lord had cautioned and was lying at the bottom of a spiritual mountain, but this time not instantly healed. There was the stunned realization of having fallen, and there was a crippling and bruising within my soul when realizing the fall had come about through fear and doubting God's plan for me. The temptation was to follow my own plan to live a quiet life with few challenges even though having vowed to serve the Lord. I still loved Him, but life in this dimension had cast a shadow, and self prevented me seeing Him as clearly as before. That was primarily due to fear of a changing world and the need for understanding his holiness. I had seen Jesus as overwhelming love, peace, and joy, but love does not just live with peace and joy. Love also lives and rules with justice and holiness. Accepting this required a hard climb upward unless

God's Word would give me wings as eagles and
before me. That required believing the Holy Spirit
give me strength for faith in God's Word, as I had
my first fall.

However, lying still and observing life from th
bottom of this mountain was all there was energy fo
currently. I observed others who had fallen and wer
wounded but found faith to persevere and ascend
from the fall. That impressed me, but I felt that I
could not regain what was lost in fellowship and
could not forgive myself. Peter knew this well and
overcame it through Jesus. Some of those falling over
the cliff were recognized. They were friends who had
betrayed our friendship. They had wanted to take
what God had given me and see me as competition.
However, they had also given of themselves to others
with encouragement and love, and to receive love,
whether for recognition or sincerely. I was not to
judge, for in judging others' faults, we find the same
unseen faults being revealed in us. Keeping my love
for them was to be continued, but the Holy Spirit
cautioned not to resume an unwise trusting bond
that infringed upon my relationship with the Lord.
Repenting and forgiving brought freedom and peace.
I prayed for deliverance from deception for all God's
creation, for it was a step towards return.

"If you will return, O Israel" says the LORD, "Return to Me, and if you will put your abominations out of my sight, then you shall not be moved, and you will swear, "The LORD lives, in truth, in judgment, and in righteousness. The nations shall bless themselves in Him, and in Him they shall glory." (Jeremiah 4:1–2)

As I forgave, there was strength to get up and obey the Holy Spirit in hopes of receiving my "wings." "Those who wait upon the Lord will rise up with wings of eagles, they will run and not grow weary, they will walk and not faint" (Isaiah 40:31).

I was sent for a sabbatical in Sedona, to my mother's house, to the area from where I had fallen, for a period of prayer and fasting for three months. There the challenge was to confront the fear and doubt that had brought me over the cliff. I could not understand why God allowed brutality and control by evil dictators, allowing abuse of children, beheadings, and hate to rule over hearts and lives. The assignment was to read of the evils of old—in the historian Josephus's accounts of battles between kingdoms annihilating one another, the Old Testament, and

testimonies of surviving persecution. History and the Bible have content that is difficult to absorb that humankind could perpetrate such horrible acts of killing for power and wealth. But there are also the stories of those who kept faith to overcome.

When the period of study was almost over, Jesus asked if I would still follow Him. As Peter once replied, "There is nowhere else to go." Someday we will have the light of understanding and know how He uses calamity for restoration. However, until then, we come to learn in life that we can trust Him to be with us, and He overcomes evil. I knew I could not lose Him again through hesitating to finish the race. I had to surrender myself to return to Him fully, and home. Restoration does not come in a day. I had to come out of my cocoon of fear to be changed to get my wings. I must inform you that the battles never cease for me, but they are for strengthening my faith.

The cover on a puzzle box can be challenging as we try to visualize what lies inside to be constructed like the picture. When we open the lid, we behold a jumble of pieces of the picture. Different shapes and colors, some bright, and some bearing no resemblance to the picture, but they are part of the whole. Those who do puzzles as a hobby know where to begin, and how to find pieces that fit together. God is teaching us how to find and put together the pieces of our lives within ourselves, and to fit to one another through love, respect, and grace.

There were still questions and a sense of losing hope of returning after coming home from the sabbatical. The Holy Spirit took over and gently touched my heart when listening to praise music. One day at a time, I was being led to scriptures that He chose and was hearing inspirational messages by different people of God that He had chosen, instead of my own choices. Those given had an illumination on things where more insight was needed. He always knew what was needed in my life. Yes, there were corrective scriptures and prophetic warnings, along with advances in understanding Him more. He kept His promise that "if" I returned, I could know anything I wanted to know. There had been teaching Sunday school classes and having spoken for Him, but the sweetness of returning was knowing Him in depth, for it was a personal relationship as a husband and wife. There was the hope of experiencing returning to the depth of love I had known. There is a time to share and a time of keeping. However, the piece of the puzzle to returning was found when I was directed to watch a few videos of life after death experiences. Although different in some respects, there were definite messages of love and truth to bring back to humankind. After two or three, a flood of my own veiled experience came back. With it came a return to the glory and overflowing love and faith of being back in the eternal dimension and the assignment to bring that kingdom here on earth. I had returned and had wings to fly again (but my flights are often canceled by spiritual weather conditions.)

Not only remembering the drawing to the kingdom above, but today, listening to vibrant praise at home, I was remembering how He had moved upon me in the past pages of my life here in our present dimension. There has been hesitation to share a couple of those, except to rejoice with you in how we can experience heaven here on earth. I did not enter heaven's gates there, but He reminded me of all the times He had allowed me to watch Him work His miracles from His mercy and grace, and to tell you to open your heart to remember yours. You do have them, even if you haven't counted or have discounted them.

Years ago, I was singing along with others in church one Sunday when I felt a separation from this dimension that I knew to be originating from the Holy Spirit opening a window that others were not seeing, but it was for me to see heaven moving on earth, instead of the ugliness of hate and war that assaults our minds and hearts as the media reports the harshness of life around the world. It was removed from my mind that day and was secure with God there in the present and not expecting anything unusual. I was not desiring anything to disturb my contentment. That's why He sent it, for there was a need to be stirred, to step into the eternal joy of God's kingdom, and to join Him in His work on earth.

The fog that precedes leaving this present reality began to act, as when we receive anesthesia before surgery. I began entering the supernatural world and was greeted with a scene of nature's bright and beautiful blue sky, but heaven's light without a sun, and the tremendous beauty of a deep gorge, rimmed by remarkably high cliffs. On their crest were forests of tall trees. Carved out in the valley far below flowed a peaceful, winding, glistening silver river, seeming to reflect the joy of what I was listening to from above the cliffs, and beneath, and in every detail of creation. To my amazement, the trees were singing praises to God. Down below, the rocks were crying out with shouts of praise. Flowers and all nature was rejoicing in the scene, and while listening to this joyful choir, there was amazement of my observing it. While watching in awe of what Jesus said would happen if he were not praised—that the rocks would cry out (Luke 19:40)—I began to feel myself zooming down, in the spirit, to the water's edge. A beautiful, soft pink water lily was awaiting me to enter its bloom. It was another world, and there was a shock to my senses to believe that I was now part of it and was praising God in song with it. Shortly afterward, the window began to close, and I returned to the church service. There was no sharing this experience for fear of being thought crazy. I was in subdued shock for a while. Had I witnessed to it, how blessed would it have been to those for whom it was sent. Our church probably would have received it; however, I lacked the courage to share it. Although the person next to me observed something happening to me and asked what had occurred, I did not share it. However, our Lord desired that I witness it to you. For confirmation, it happened to other NDE people, to see nature rejoicing in heaven. God does not waste His blessings. He doesn't give up on us to fulfill our purpose when we trip over an opportunity, or our pride, in our path in life. He is there to keep us from falling over a cliff. Remember, His everlasting arms are under you.

There was the time when asked to volunteer at the local cancer center as chaplain that the Holy Spirit told me I was to go to a trailer park in the area and would be sent to pray for a woman who had cancer, but I was cautioned that someone there might be a problem. The next day, my director asked me to go to the trailer park in that location and pray for and comfort the lady there suffering with cancer but was told she might have been sent to the hospital. She had been sent, and I went to the hospital. When stopping at the door to enter the room, she began to cry out in amazement, and her children looked shaken and left us to have privacy. While still standing there at the doorway, I was aware that the precious presence of Jesus was beside me. She exclaimed that she saw Jesus walk in with me, and she was overcome with emotion. I went to her and prayed with her as I had been told. She had bone cancer, but she got out of bed and was able to walk, which amazed the doctors. She called me afterward, crying that they wanted her to take chemo, but she knew that Jesus had healed her. She begged me to tell them she was healed. Not knowing what to do, as I would not go against her doctors, I reluctantly told her to do what she thought was best. She submitted to the chemo and died one year later. Upon hearing about her death, sorrow filled me, and there was blame for myself for not standing with her. I went to the trailer to comfort the family. There, slumped over outside against the trailer, sat her grieving husband, deep in grief. We talked, and he admitted how he had ignored her hope for him, his treatment of her, and his drinking. It had not caused him to change while she was alive, but now he was alone, and she was a good woman, a good wife. He was depressed and ashamed. I told him about God's forgiveness and how she prayed for him to accept Jesus Christ's gift of salvation. He repented of his behavior and was comforted and began restoration. When seeing her children later, they reported he became a changed man and attended church. She would have given her life to see him restored. However, visiting her often to encourage and strengthen her faith during that year could have encouraged faith, and hope, and restored healing. We can be too busy with our lives to follow up. However, she had to make the decision to believe for her healing, and it was not my place to make it for her. The hospital called me the next day after Jesus came to heal her. They said they would send a van to bring me to the hospital to convince her to take the chemo. Of course I would not. We all have a decision to make when people do not believe Jesus can heal or guide our decisions. But we can fortify our courage to stand up to the pressures of humankind. This testimony is for us to realize our responsibility to complete our assignments. God must reveal both blessings and our falls from grace, for time requires our diligence to keep the covenant we made with Him. There have been missed chances to witness, and I do not always fulfill my assignments, so the Holy Spirit told me clearly to write my witness and give it to those who might accept it.

God does not only want us to return to Him, but to return to who He made us to become, that we might be secure in His love, and in our true identity, to experience the joy of living, of giving, of loving, and of knowing the privilege of creating heaven on earth with Him.

I had not felt my true self for a long time, even after being revived. The world wants, sometimes, and for selfish reasons, to create us in their image, to become a unity of mind and goals; that is, a "one fit all," and it can pull us from our course and our destined identity. I had been secretly searching for myself, for it was if I was not wearing the right shoes, feeling discomfort from my reactions to life.

One day there was an urge to open a closed and forgotten desk drawer that had not been opened in years. I picked up a thick green notebook that felt like a forgotten friend, which held intimate sharing with Jesus, riches of knowledge, and scripture's interpretations. Insights from the Holy Spirit beyond my present cognizance. I read the pages with the thrill of discovering buried treasure, wondering who had written them but recognizing the "brush strokes" that declared my identity. There was found the soul that had been lost for a while, a different version of today, and one that Jesus wanted to return to Him. That soul knew Him well enough, with no reluctance to follow wherever the path might lead. We cannot truly return to God until returning to the one who He has been creating. We must desire for Him to continue, for we are not yet a finished product.

People everywhere are struggling to find identity, to know where they fit, where they really belong. Your identity is in Him who created you. I pray for us to look for Him, to seek His light and His Truth. To know we will be continuing to be created throughout eternity. We don't give up on us for He has the ability, and the pleasure, of re-creating what we have messed up.

We are entering a Valley of Decision that we might have been traveling for a long time. But the sand in the hourglass is running out, and then time will be no more (Revelation 10:5–7).

I want to thank Jesus for saving me to take you with me to revisit that eternal dimension, and that it is true reality. God is real, heaven is real, and it is the home we have longed for. God is in control over the good and the bad in this world and our lives. As we debate and hesitate, heaven is waiting for our decision. I pray my obedience in writing this witness will help you make the right one.

Epilogue

I visited the place of my fall and miracle healing just once at West Fork in Oak Creek Canyon, Arizona. It was thirty years after the event. It was not on my agenda for I had gone to Sedona for other reasons that had to be addressed. However, God knew it was time for a return to recall His faithfulness and belief in miracles. I had gone there with two friends.

One was my loving but cautioning friend Peg, who I invited to go with me to the Red Rocks. She was a delightful personality. She was one you knew you could trust with your admissions of struggling with everyday confrontations. Her lanky gait of confident seeking for her assignments or rushing to assist those hurting was a profile of a sister called to prayer and service. We had fellowship and laughter when driving to engage with a ministry which came to our church asking for volunteers to minister to the homeless and drug addicts. We felt the call from the Lord to accept the challenge, and I have never regretted it.

The days of praying for the homeless and the memories of Williams Street were a special time for me of realizing our Creator's heart for those who had lost the path to finding hope. Peg and I had the same compassion for the homeless who were without their own bed, their own privacy, and clinging to their pride to continue to hope the next day would be better and their chances would change. We were somewhat surprised at what we found. We rode in a renovated school bus with a makeshift kitchen in the back containing hot meals for the homeless and Williams Street ministry. The days of praying for the homeless and the memories of Williams Street were an awakening that affects my life to this day.

We arrived in Dayton to find a few homeless members awaiting our arrival. They were clean and expectant as they marched across the pavement, wearing almost new clothing. They climbed the steps into the school bus ready for a hot meal, and later to search through the ministry van for articles of clothes, shoes, and whatever the treasures of that week.

I recall an excited young man making his way down the aisle, bubbling in anticipation to inform the two women overseeing the meals in the makeshift kitchen in the back that their prayers were answered, and he had been admitted into a school for college courses. As a matronly lady and her husband climbed the steps clothed as if they were going out to dine in an excellent restaurant, I had to reevaluate my concept of homelessness. The couple had been previously employed at Dayton's cash register plant, which had shut down, and their finances were eliminated. They had lost the luxuries of boats and cars. However, they were pleasant, calm, and expectant as they appreciated that friends had come to help them in their plight.

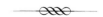

From visiting the homeless, the bus departed for Williams Street. We prayed silently as we knew the dangers and had to be prepared. The school bus would park alongside a large square which was favored with a lone, robust, towering maple tree. But it was surrounded with expended needles flung there from the drug users. We were parked under the shade of this large tree to shield from the summer sun. A row of shabby houses on the right of the square was a gathering place for those shooting up. No houses across the street and abandoned buildings on the south side of the square. Boarded fence north of the square. They were out on their porches unashamedly shooting up.

The meals were ready for those who would come to eat hot and delicious food. We had an array of doughnuts, which they seemed to prefer if we brought to them as they were gathering around the bus. Some came for the food, but most were too busy with the drugs. I remember walking across the square to bring doughnuts to a man wandering around because my "mother instinct" went into gear, over caution, and I wanted him to enjoy the treats we brought while Alan went to their porches to talk to and pray for them. They were familiar with him as he understood them and their struggles, giving a weekly message behind a wooden pulpit and bringing a songstress to touch their hearts.

I approached this big man and asked him, "Sir, would you like a doughnut?" I felt God had a reason for approaching him despite the danger and addressing him in a term with which he was not familiar. He seemed startled by being addressed as "Sir," but he took the doughnut with a look of surprise. As I looked up into his face, I saw the emptiness and effects of the drugs, but I was not afraid for God had a shield around me for this assignment. I felt no threat because we were establishing a trust needed to reach into their souls.

I turned to walk away, but before I had crossed the square, he became like an insane person and began to call out a garbled incoherency of words and was waving his arms above his head. I saw the protection I had been given to see the emptiness and effect of the drugs, and I knew God wanted him to feel he was respected by calling him "Sir," and to pray for him. They desire respect more than drugs. I had to see their world for the urgency of intercession. I had been locked into my world of church and the comfort of home.

My courage was tested as I was offering doughnuts to those lingering around the bus. I turned to encounter a tall Black man leaning over my shoulder, peering down at me. His eyes were blood red, and the pupils were like black projectiles staring intensely back at me. I saw the demon of addiction inside. It was like envisioning a chained soul within him, where aggression lurked and wanted to lunge at this unwanted intruder. He might have but for a comrade behind him who tugged at his T-shirt. He lost interest and walked away without a word.

You ask why I would take the risk. Because I was sent and because David looked into the face of a giant and knew he was sent to face evil and overcome it, and we are sent with the power Jesus acquired for us at a heavy price. God used my naivety; common sense would have refused to go. But that taught me to use common sense afterward, and I canceled one trip to minister, as a lovely young woman signed up to go with us, for I knew I was to stay home and pray hard. I learned that she had forgotten protective footwear to carefully avoid the needles within their territory. Looking back, I wonder why the needles were not taken away. Perhaps because we were in their territory and not invited. The new volunteer wore thin sandals. As she stepped out of the bus and onto the square, she was stepping onto a needle. One of the addicts who had come to eat, immediately grabbed her foot and pulled the needle out before it entered her foot. Showing our respect for them as God's creations brought about their protective attitude.

I remember seeing a neighborhood woman who was walking briskly down the sidewalk toward me as I was being drawn to stroll toward her, feeling I knew her in the spirit, a sister who was there for the same reason. We automatically came together in an embrace, and there were three of us as the Holy Spirit was there to meet with us. She exuded a victorious joy in having been delivered from her own addiction. She was from the neighborhood and just leaving church to come to bring the presence of the Holy Spirit to spill over into their lostness. They needed her to bring hope, and she needed to bring her freedom to liberate them from their addiction.

Apparently, it did, as a beautiful young lady sang before Alan gave the message. Her song filled the atmosphere with a sweet promise of freedom and a whispering call to decision. I moved needles from under the sheltering tree from the hot and humid summer day to sit uncaring of the hard earth beneath me because the Holy Spirit swept over me and moved me with compassion to pray for them. Tears rolled down my cheeks, and I was noticed by our audience, observing the songstress, and apparently me, from their porches. However, I was not aware of their notice.

Suddenly, there was a gentle movement at my right side. I became aware of an old, bearded Black man, wearing a cap over his white hair, who sat down beside me, leaning over to gaze in wonder at my tears. I continued praying in intercession, and he knew it was for him and the others. When the invitation went forth, he rose to his feet and humbly, with head held high, walked determinedly forward to receive Jesus as his Savior.

He was not the only one who felt the touch of the Holy Spirit on his soul. A mature woman, probably in her late fifties, wearing scrubs, and just coming home from work, walked slowly toward the wooden pulpit to answer the call to salvation. She was bringing her young grandchild with her, holding his hand. I had not recognized her presence before. I went to her afterward, and we talked about her life there. She said that when you have always known the life of drugs, and if it is the acceptable life around you, it is natural to realize there is no way of escape. Her grandchild changed that for her. She wanted a better future for him. However, when you are lost in the barricades of walls of addiction, and you find the gates are opening, you learn that Jesus has the keys.

Do I believe love can overcome lostness? Yes, I do, when we give it. Jesus gives it through us!

Then there was Ernie. Sometimes Alan would drive the bus through the neighborhood, and we would give candy to the children while Alan told them about Jesus. He would then drive into a field where he parked, to minister to some neighborhood folk. Peg and I got off and stood over to the right of the field where he was talking to the people and praying for them. We heard the rattle of a large, dated Oldsmobile come chugging across the field to stop behind us. Someone who had been with the ministry before Peg and I came along, turned with a dreaded groan to mumble, "Here comes Ernie!"

He came with eagerness for a battle of wits with these Christians who thought they knew their Bible. He came prepared, as he studied the Bible, not to agree with it or confirm it through testimony, but to find a loophole to defend his drunken lifestyle. He came also with his mental boxing gloves on. He was a large roly-poly individual, with an arm hanging out of the window of his beloved Oldsmobile, and grinning in anticipation of declaring victory over us with his keen mind. He obviously had a little too much of his bottle, eager to enter a spiritual boxing ring with us. The Holy Spirit was waiting for Ernie's visit, and God loved him and had humor in Ernie's effort to escape acknowledging Him. That would mean giving up his bottle of drink that kept him medicated and happy—medicated from hidden wounds he bore and pain he could not escape. He had to conquer the fear that God and the Bible were true.

We entered the "ring," and the first bout was about Noah having gotten drunk when leaving the ark. He targeted me for the battle and tried to land a punch that Noah was no better than he. I found myself having loving compassion for him, and my "boxing gloves" were soft but firm, and the counterpunches landed, and his face emitted a surprised reaction that he could not duck the truth of God's Word. I enjoyed the confrontation he was having with the Holy Spirit, and I believed he recognized that the battle wasn't with me but the Holy Spirit.

He fought to keep his bottle, for his bottle was his best friend, perhaps his only friend. It kept him from the losses in his life and longing for things and dreams he could not obtain. God knew how tightly he was holding onto deception and self, but He knew who would win the final bout.

I wasn't there to see the continuing fight to overcome these Christians; however, I was there when he came back the next week to try once more. He had weakened and was a little afraid to debate, so I hope and pray he lost the trophy to the Holy Spirit when our time of ministry was over.

I am remembering Ernie once again as I write, and the many Ernies fighting God and those who believe in the Bible, and we need to pray for them. God will take the sting of their criticism if we give them the love of God and continue to stand for truth.

Returning to West Fork in Oak Creek Canyon

After my mother's death, who I brought home to live with me when she displayed the symptoms of Alzheimer's, there was a challenge to begin with starting the process of dealing with my mother's vacant home, having promised her I would not sell. Dreading going to her house without her there, I needed someone to go with me. Peg came to mind strongly, and I was comfortable with her personality. I was uncertain of a positive answer for her leaving for two weeks, knowing she had a busy life, and going on a trip with me probably would not fit into her schedule. Apparently, God had chosen her because she was free at that time but debated on leaving her husband. They discussed the invitation to adventure to the Red Rocks, and he consented, and she agreed.

Ted, my other companion on the hike that day, was not a typical person I would have thought to be interested in hiking with me. We were opposite types, and he was both friend and adversary. He had come into my mother's life three weeks after my brother's death. Hal had lived with her for eleven years, leaving life in California after my father passed away. They were close companions. Her garage roof needed repair after the storm, and her friend Eve recommended Ted as a carpenter.

Mother was grieving as she stood at the door watching him work. It reminded her of Hal working there for her. He was tall, like my brother, but had a quite different personality. She saw something in him that needed to be healed, plus being there without anyone to help take care of the repairs. She had never lived alone. Family always surrounded her. I had asked her to live with me in Ohio, but she loved Sedona. Her home was her castle, and she could not leave it. Besides, she said God had an assignment for her there in the West. I could not get her to agree to assistance to living alone, and she faced her fear and the challenge. She found that she loved her independence and enjoyed her porch under the sheltering mulberry trees, except she missed her son. They had ministered together for a healing ministry, and she loved working together. Adopting a carpenter seemed an answer to Hal's prayer for her to continue to live in the house she loved. God knew Ted was someone who needed a mother figure in his life to heal his brokenness of divorce and losing being with his daughter, and she needed someone to fill the vacancy in her heart. So without suspecting it, Ted became adopted and became her assignment.

He was not the kind to want to be adopted. He had a disagreeable, grumpy personality, was very independent and had been a roaming hippie type in earlier years. But Mom cooked delicious meals for him while he worked. He fought against becoming her "family," but when she "adopted" his daughter, who loved her, he relented. He grew to love my mother. He was still grumpy with her when she wanted him to do small repairs, and he complained and grumped. When I was there for visits, my feathers were ruffled. I let him know I did not like how he fussed with my mother, but Mom did not mind; he was her "assignment."

Ted had adventured over much of the United States and Mexico looking for pleasures and excitement for the adventure. C. S. Lewis speaks to this illusion of searching to find the place where we will find we will be satisfied with all the things we dream to acquire, and where we will find happiness and a home where we belong. They find themselves in a dead end and begin searching for another path that leads nowhere, all leading to unfulfillment, for when they get to the end of the paths and the end of adventure, it is empty.

Friends can turn into betrayal, and sins lead into sickness of soul and body. So Ted's attitude was to mistrust, to be angry, to grumble and complain. The only treasure he had found was his beautiful and talented daughter, whom he dearly loved and protected. She eventually became the granddaughter that mother so needed, as she missed seeing her grandchildren grow up, except for vacations. So Mom got her wish for family. Ted mellowed under Mom's loving hands and telling him about God's love, but God still had work to do, as in all of us. I finally accepted him as part of the family.

When mother died here in Ohio, I had to go to Sedona and take care of repairs. There was a need for someone to tear out and rebuild. Who to hire but Mom's grumpy "adopted" son, who she would have wanted to rebuild her house. When Peg and I arrived in Arizona, Ted came to discuss the job. Peg and Ted became instant friends. He decided to take Peg on a guided tour of the Red Rocks. I sat in the back of Mom's Mustang because Ted's truck was full of clutter. They sang songs from Elvis Presley and the Beatles, and it was amusing listening to these "singing birds," which was not my style. However, it was surprising to see Ted behaving from debating and making his grievances known. Peg was loving the adventure to all the Indian ruins and a picnic to admire the Sedona sunset. However, our fried chicken attracted some wildlife, and Ted told us to get into his truck, which he cleaned out for the picnic. He detected a crackling sound in the weeds and heavy breathing, which were alerts that perhaps a mountain lion wanted to join our picnic. Ted had told me once about adventures of hiking and camping in the Superstition Mountains. When I asked if anything unusual happened, as there had been stories told of supernatural events for some who had hiked and camped there, he seemed to hesitate on relaying one event that apparently haunted him.

He had been camping in the mountains and zipped up in his sleeping bag. He woke in the night to the horror of having his sleeping bag dragged around, and he heard the growling of a large animal. It lasted for a while, and he feared for his life. After a while, it stopped the dragging and everything became quiet. He lay there trembling in the sleeping bag, fearing the bag would be torn apart, leaving him to face what had been dragging him. At dawn he emerged to look for signs of the battle in the dust around the bag. He was shocked to find there was no trace of an animal's footprints in the loose dirt. It had not been a dream, as he was fully awake. He had no answer for what had happened, and the mystery of the experience seemed to trouble this adventurer of the West.

He took us to Jerome upon the mountain, which was a prominent copper mine long ago. We ate at the Haunted Hamburger, and the legend of hauntings flourished in Jerome. I asked the adventuring Ted if he had ever experienced any unusual occurrences there. He had stayed for a time in the hotel that was supposedly haunted, and he admitted to believing in the stories, as the window would open and close, and sounds were heard all through the night. However, I had my doubts, and it could all be manipulated for tourists. People seem to enjoy fearing the unknown, for we are drawn to mystery. However the mysteries of God's eternal realm are those we should contemplate, for God wants us to seek Him and to know Him.

Ted informed us we were going to West Fork. I had not known that was in the plan, as I had not been back in thirty years. I would then revisit my special visit to the place of what had, and would, continue to change my life.

We were friends with different personalities but who accepted one another as pieces of the puzzle of life. That day is a page in my memories, as Ted had cancer about three years later and had stubbornly continued to work despite the pain to pay his rent. We had our last difference of opinion when he was in the hospital, and I wanted him to see a beloved person in his life that he was rejecting. He gave in, I am sure, because love always wins. But he remained opinionated until the end. He would always be Ted, and that was all right. He fully accepted Jesus before he died but had to fuss at Him to get his viewpoint in.

When we arrived at West Fork, it had changed over the years. There was a new bridge over Oak

Creek, and the creek naturally had changes in its volume, and maybe a little of its course from the surge from the mountains at that time of year. I told him of the event I had experienced there. He seemed to doubt that it had occurred in this place. However, I pressed down the path to find the mountain slope I had climbed. He argued that there was no mountain where I said it was. He didn't like competition of his guidance and knew he was right, and I was wrong. However, I saw the mountain as we were hiking around a curve in the path. When I spoke about the road above the abutment where we were parked, he said there was no road there. Then he remembered there had been at one time.

We stopped to take a picture of a little gopher right in the middle of the path, who seemed glad to have his work being noticed in digging a deeper hole. We found the chimney, and I looked across the creek to see the place where my fall had occurred. The years of erosion had cut the distance in half, and now the creek was full. That dampened my hope to see the area would look the same. It made my fall look like a tumble.

Things change, and people change. Time can dim or erase memories of events if we only look at the changing culture and the changing environments. Someone not of faith might wonder in some unbelief how three wise men would leave their countries to follow a star to find a king who was born into this world from another dimension. And how could that babe grow up to save us from a fall that separated humankind from God, until God sent His Son (that infant king), to save us from the consequences from the Fall.

I believe it because it happened to me!

"Tapestry"

BY SHIRLEY STOLL

The rivers have gouged deeper and reshaped the land in places, but as I cross them again in thought, they bring past, present, and future into focus, stirring the depths of my heart.

Sounds that were are silent now, voices of the past that I strain to hear are no longer within the radius of my listening ear. They are no longer here but are in other worlds of thinking, growing, and dimensions of living. They are gone from my protective embrace, released to the Lord.

They are touched by different impressions, received trace elements of a different composition. Were created as a unique expression of beauty and form. Yet they would become part of all that God has created and become part of Him.

They would be blended by the hand of God, with faith, hope, and love so they could be changed from the face of "conformity" to human design and formed into the image of His Grace.

But where did all the voices go, and the hopes I had for them, and they had for themselves? Where does their river flow after so many years of sun and rain, drought, and stormy days here in this dimension?

Why, these voices are speaking from the same souls, within the dimension their rivers of life have forged into. They are busily moving in and out of the fabric of life, following the Master's hand.

Shakings come, and decisions are made, which determine the course and flow of our lives. The river flashes in the sun like a silver needle, drawing along the thread of our attitudes and beliefs, through a "living tapestry." Living because it captures every note of every song we have ever sung, as well as the weaving of every thread.

And so the needle moves ahead, piercing through

territory yet to be lived. We follow, after having been driven through the eye of the needle. We must follow; we can but flow with it.

The needle draws us through the fabric until the color needs change, due to the Master's design.

Then, once again we are driven through the eye of the needle and continue to dip under circumstances, and are brought up and out, only to go under once again, and yet to merge in the course of time with the pattern of the picture.

So why should we tremble? Isn't it all in the will of the Master designer, and will He not reveal the design of His plan to those who are called by His name?

Everything changes, but yesterday's faith brings new shape to today's doubts. The threads of yesterday are woven into today's challenges. And today will decide and be part of tomorrow.

To endure, to persevere, and believe makes the tapestry full of color and challenge to the end.

And should we be disappointed in the picture, we must remember, the colors were chosen by us. If the grays and blacks predominate, was it not the choice of disbelief over the choice of faith in God, or of anger and doubt over joy and trust?

And when the shades of night are being woven all around us, we need not fear. The night has not won with its darkness; the Holy Spirit is here to make our lamp to shine, to weave golden threads in the tapestry.

"Watchman, watchman, what of the night?"

"Hush your fears. The night is outside yourself. Arise and shine, the light has come."

Doctor's reported of complaining because I was brought in for evaluation. I was full of joy!

Name: *Shirley M. Stoll*   Date of Birth: *8–7–37*

Dependent of: *Albert W. Stoll*

Address: xxxxxxxxxxxxxxxxxxxxxxxxxxxx
Phone: *xxxxxxx*

P: 1. Scalp laceration
    2. Concussion
    3. Significant thyroid nodule.
D: 1. Repair laceration
    2. Head sheet given to family, close observation, recheck in 24 hrs.
    3. Must follow up on return to Ohio.

PI: Patient was hiking in Oak Creek, frightened by a snake, slipped and fell approximately 10 feet landing on a rock. Those with her state she was unconscious for approximately 10 minutes and then became responsive remembering all the events of the day. She had an ??? scalp laceration and was brought to the office for examination. ???ed of pain and swelling of the right elbow.

PE: Alert, well oriented lady who is in moderate distress complaining of discomfort in the head of pain and swelling of the right elbow.

PE: Alert, well oriented lady who is in moderate distress complaining of discomfort in the head and the right elbow. Blood pressure 120/80, pulse is 80 and regular. The pupils are equal and reactive, the optic discs are quite sharp and very normal. No blood behind TM's. Neck supple, heart RSR, no murmur. A stellate laceration in the right parietal area, it extends down to the skull (which is normal to palpation). The remainder of neurologic examination is normal.

Procedure: Under local anesthesia the laceration was debrided and closed utilising 4-0 silk in the galia and in the skin. Patient and husband are advised to have sutures removed in one week. Husband is given a copy of head injury sheet with instructions to evaluate her frequently during the night and return in the a.m.

8–9–80: Patient did quite well during the night with no difficulties and feels quite well this morning.

PE: Eyegrounds again are quite normal, grip strength equal R & L, wound check, looks good. Patient considered well enough to return to Ohio tomorrow.

Printed in the United States
by Baker & Taylor Publisher Services